100 + Fun Ideas

Teaching PE Games

Adela de Castro Mangas

Brilliant
PUBLICATIONS

Other Titles in the 100+ Fun Ideas Series:

Published by Brilliant Publications
Unit 10, Sparrow Hall Farm
Edlesborough, Dunstable
Bedfordshire, LU6 2ES, UK
www.brilliantpublications.co.uk

General information enquiries:
Tel: 01525 222292

The name Brilliant Publications and the
logo are registered trademarks.

Written by Adela de Castro Mangas
Cover ilustration: Pat Murray
Illustrations: Narcea, SA de Ediciones

© Design Brilliant Publications 2011

Printed ISBN 978-1-905780-84-6

First printed and published in the UK in
2011

Originally published in Spain in 2007 by
Narcea, SA de Ediciones, with the title,
Juegos para Educatión Física.

Contents

Strength games 87–97

Winding-down games......
.... 98–110

Teaching PE Games

Introduction

A child at play displays imagination and spontaneity. Playing games develops a child's skills at teamwork, co-operation and socializing.

This book has been written by a practising PE teacher and includes many tried-and–tested games that children have enjoyed playing. Playing not only hones children's physical skills, it also strengthens their emotional well-being.

Aims of this book

This book is intended to provide practical teaching materials for use in PE lessons. The games can easily be adapted to suit other situations, such as after school clubs and the winding-down games can be used at any time during the school day, as part of a transition exercise, or part of a lesson. The activities can be modified to take differing children's needs into consideration; indeed you may find that when a group is introduced to a new game, they make their own modifications and adjustments to the rules.

This book of games for developing physical skills is for anyone to use and enjoy; teacher, child, parent, adult. It is not necessary to be a 'great athlete' to participate successfully in any of these games; what is important is having a go and joining in. The activities are suitable for any age group.

How to use this book

This book includes over 100 games, all of which develop basic physical skills, and they are divided into chapters according to those skills. The games also have secondary benefits. For example, many of the games designed to help co-ordination also develop agility, and many of the speed games develop both co-ordination and agility .

The games are grouped as follows:

Chapter	Skill
1	Agility
2	Co-ordination
3	Resistance
4	Speed
5	Strength
6	Winding-down

In each game the most appropriate age group for use is indicated. This is just a recommendation and you should vary it according to the needs of the group you are working with.

The skill or skills being developed are shown in each game as well. When carrying out and completing the games, we recommend taking the following steps:

1. Introduce the game: motivate the pupils to participate from the very start
2. Specify the playing area
3. Set up the groups or teams
4. Explain how to play the game including any rules
5. Evaluate the results.

This last step only needs to be done by the teacher, although sometimes for educational purposes the pupils may be involved. Please remember that the success will depend on each participating individual's abilities as well as the objectives for the game.

Playing always consists of reciprocal pupil-teacher learning and must never exclude any pupils; it should encourage respect, responsibility, and co-operation.

Each and every game is adaptable and interactive; they complement each other and so are easily combined.

Chapter 1
Agility games

Agility is our capacity to quickly and effectively change direction whilst moving at speed.

It is the ability a person has to set off and cover short distances quickly and with precision.

How agile we are depends on our co-ordination and strength.

Agility can improve how well we socialize, make friends and collaborate. It can also help reduce our fears and inhibitions.

These games test the body's ability to make changes of direction, sudden stops and quick starts, have fast reaction times, and so on.

1. **Divided we stand!** 6+

Co-ordination/speed **Equipment:** *Soft balls*

✦ Split the children into two teams: A and B.

✦ Divide team A in half and stand them at either ends of the playing area with team B standing in the space between.

✦ The aim is for the players at the ends to hit those in the middle using the soft balls. The players in the middle must dodge any balls coming in their direction and avoid being hit. They must not catch/kick the balls.

✦ Any player taking a hit is out. The game finishes when all the players are out, or an allotted time has passed.

✦ After each game the teams swap roles.

Safety note: Set an acceptable target zone, such as below the knee. Keep the numbers of children in each team limited so there are not too many balls being thrown at any one time.

Teaching PE Games

2. **Who will get there?** 6+

Co-ordination/speed **Equipment:** *A whistle/hooter*

✦ All of the players stand behind a line at one end of the playing area.

✦ When the teacher blows the whistle, the players start walking as fast as they can forwards, without running. When the whistle blows again, they must stop.

✦ On the next whistle, they begin to walk backwards. Each time the whistle blows they must change from walking forwards, stopping or walking backwards, to the next move in the sequence until one of them reaches the other end of the playing area.

✦ Players will be out for not following instructions or for running.

Variations: Include verbal, audible, or visual signals. Use repeated signals so the children must remember the sequence of moves or different signals for each move: forward, backward and stop.

3. **Catch the snake** 6+

Co-ordination/speed/resistance   ***Equipment:*** *Ropes 2m in length*

✦   Divide the children into two groups: shakers and stampers.

✦   The shakers hold one end of a rope loosely between their thumb and index finger and make it move along the floor like a snake.

✦   While the shakers run around the playing area trailing the rope behind them, the stampers try to step on the rope to make the shakers drop it.

✦   If a stamper steps on the rope and it falls on the floor, the roles are swapped.

Variations: It is possible to change the number of shakers and stampers in the game. The game can also be played in pairs.

4. Look, no hands! 6+

Co-ordination/balance/co-operation **Equipment:** *Large soft balls, hoops*

✦ Divide children into pairs.

✦ Place some balls within the hoops.

✦ Each pair must run up to the hoop together and try to remove the ball without using their hands. They must always work together.

✦ Decide whether the ball just needs to be removed from the hoop or, to make it harder, moved to another area/hoop etc.

✦ The pair that manages the task the fastest, wins.

5. Knees 'n' ankles   6+

Balance/fast reaction

✦   The players stand in pairs, facing each other.

✦   The aim of each player is to try to touch the knee of their partner, without their own knee being touched.

Variation: Try to touch ankles whilst squatting instead of standing.

6. Knot the right person!　　　8+

Co-operation/collaboration

✦　Stand ten children in a small circle.

✦　They each join hands with two others, but making sure that it is not with the person standing right next to them.

✦　Once everyone in the group has all joined hands, they must scramble around to see if they can undo the knot they're in without letting go of their hands.

7. **Taking orders!**   8+

Speed/co-ordination   **Equipment:** *Whistle*

✦ Pupils run around the playing area but must keep listening for instructions.

✦ They must now do what the teacher says.

✦ Example: To the right of … ! And everybody must run to the right of the person named.
In front of … !
With … !
Behind … !
Far away from … !
To the left of … !

8. **Blind guards** 8+

Co-ordination/speed/reflexes   ***Equipment:*** *2 blindfolds, 1 chair*

✦ Sort children into groups of five.

✦ From each group of five, one child is the prisoner and is seated on a chair, two children are guards and the last two are the rescuers trying to save the prisoner.

✦ The two guards are blindfolded, and must try to stop the prisoner being freed by tagging the rescuers while they quietly try to reach the prisoner.

✦ To free the prisoner, a rescuer must tag the prisoner.

✦ Swap roles after each game.

9. **Lace-chase** 7+

Co-ordination/reflexes

✦ This game consists of trying to undo the shoelaces of the other players, whilst avoiding them undoing yours.

NB: If not all children have shoelaces, then use ribbon tied around their ankles.

10. **Step on it!** 7+

Speed/co-ordination/reflexes

✦ This activity consists of stepping on all the other player's feet, whilst avoiding being stepped on by one of them.

✦ The game is played in a designated area, the size of which depends on the number of players. As the number of participants decreases, the playing area could also be reduced.

✦ The game finishes when there is only one player left who hasn't been stepped on.

Safety note: Remind the children not to stamp on each other's feet; they must not get rough.

11. Dress the chair   7+

Speed/co-ordination   **Equipment:** *4 chairs, 16 handkerchiefs, 4 blindfolds*

✦   Divide the children into groups of four and number the players 1 to 4.

✦   Place a chair in the play area of the room with four handkerchiefs scattered close by.

✦   Blindfold Player 1 from the first group.

✦   With directions from his/her team-mates, Player 1 must crawl to find the four handkerchiefs and then tie each one to a different leg of the chair.

✦   Allow all Player 1s to take their turn, timing the players to reveal an overall winner.

✦   Play the Player 2s against each other and so on.

12. **Hand-balloon** 7+

Co-operation/collaboration/co-ordination   **Equipment:** *Balloons*

✦ This game is played in two teams of three, in a small designated area, with each team defending a goal at one end.

✦ The children must hit/pat a balloon with their hands to their team-mates, to try to manoeuvre the balloon to the opponent's end of the field to score a goal/point.

✦ If the balloon touches the floor, play passes over to the other team.

13. **The hunters** 8+

Co-operation/socialization/speed   **Equipment:** *Soft ball*

✦ One player acts as 'prey' and moves along the perimeter of the area. The rest of the children should be spread evenly around the playing area. They are the 'hunters'.

✦ The 'hunters' cannot move their feet. They must pass a ball to those who are closest to the prey so they can try to touch the prey with it. The ball must NOT be thrown to hit the prey.

✦ Whoever manages to hit the prey will become the prey in the next game.

Variations: More balls can be given and/or more prey.

14. **Chase the snake** 6+

Co-operation/co-ordination/speed

✦ Divide children into groups of five or six.

✦ Ask the children to make a chain by standing one behind the other and holding onto the shoulders of the person in front.

✦ The child at the front must now try to get hold of the shoulders of the last person in the chain, without anyone letting go. Meanwhile all the children in the chain must move around and try to avoid this happening.

✦ When the first child does manage to get the last player's shoulders, then they become the last of the chain and the second child in the chain takes the first place and the game begins again.

15. **Musical chairs** 6+

Speed/reflexes   **Equipment:** *Chairs, music/whistle*

✦ To start, allow the same number of chairs as students. The chairs are arranged back to back, in a row, so the seats are facing outwards.

✦ The pupils start by sitting on the chairs, then as the music starts, they must run around the chairs. When the music stops playing, the children must sit down on the first chair they find. Do a dry-run first, so no-one is out and the children understand what is expected of them.

✦ In the next round, remove a chair. The child without a seat is out.

✦ Continue the game and the one who is left sitting on the last chair is the winner.

16. Hoops take-away! 6+

Co-operation/speed **Equipment:** *Hoops, music/whistle*

✦ This game is similar to the game of 'Musical chairs' (activity 15), but it is played with hoops and in pairs.

✦ The players run around the play area in pairs.

✦ On the whistle, the pairs must find a hoop and stand in it together.

✦ The pair who do not find a hoop is out.

✦ Take away a hoop and continue to play until only one pair remain.

17. **Hoops take-away! (variation)**   6+

Companionship/collaboration/
co-ordination/speed

Equipment: *The same number of hoops*
and cones as children minus one

✦   In this variation, all the children remain in play until the last
    hoop has been played.

✦   Divide the children into pairs and set out your hoops within the
    playing area.

✦   When you blow the whistle, each pair must look for a hoop and
    stand inside it. The pair left without a hoop receives a point.
    Keep a tally chart of which pairs gain points.

✦   The game continues with all the children 'mingling' in the
    playing area. Take out a hoop each time the music stops.

✦   So, for example, after the children have played for a second time,
    there are two fewer hoops than pairs and those pairs receive a
    point each. (Most pairs are going to receive several points, as
    they will frequently miss out on getting in a hoop.)

✦   The pair that win will be the pair that has accumulated the least
    number of points on the final hoop.

18. Hot hands   6+

Time of reaction (speed)/agility

✦   In pairs facing each other, the participants join palms with palms
    (hands held out flat, one above, one below).

✦   The player who has their hands underneath tries to hit the top
    of the hands of their partner before they can react and take
    them away.

✦   It can also be played either with their finger tips touching or
    standing a small distance from each other, without touching.

Safety note: Children can tend to get a little carried away with this
game, so a few reminders may be needed about not getting too 'heavy
handed'.

19. Aye, aye Captain 6+

Speed/co-ordination

✦ Go through the list of orders that the 'crew' should be familiar with:

Clear the deck – everyone must lie on the floor with their feet off of the floor.

Scrub the deck – everyone on their knees scrubbing.

Hit the deck – everyone must lie down on their stomach.

Three men in a boat – they must form groups of three and sing 'Row, row, row your boat'.

Man-over-board – Players must find a partner as quickly as possible. One partner must lay on their stomach on the floor while the other places a foot on their partner's back.

✦ Choose one child to be captain who has to shout out orders for his/her crew. Any player not following orders is out.

Variation: Be captain yourself and use sailing vocabulary linked to an action.

Stern – back of boat

Bow – front of boat

Port – left-hand side of boat

Starboard – right-hand side of boat

Chapter 2
Co-ordination games

Co-ordination is the body's neuromuscular capacity to move the different muscle groups in a controlled way. It allows movements to be synchronized.

Gross motor co-ordination is controlled by the larger muscle masses, executing movements which require little or no precision.

Fine motor co-ordination relates to movements which require greater muscular control, particularly of the hands and feet in conjunction with sight (eye-hand and eye-foot co-ordination).

20. **Stork race**   6+

Agility/balance/collaboration

✦   Divide the children into groups of six.

✦   Each group must form a line, standing one behind the other on
       the starting line.

✦   Each child in the line must hold the ankle and the shoulder of
       the classmate in front until everyone is hooked together.

✦   All of the members of the group must start moving/hopping
       together, without letting go of each other until they reach the
       finishing line.

✦   If someone does let go, the first child must run to the back of
       their group and join up before the whole group can move again.

Variation: This game can be done with all groups competing at once or
as a timed event.

21. Shoot the bag 8+

Agility/reflexes/aim   ***Equipment:*** *Balls/beanbags, 2 x bag/bucket*

✦   Divide the children into two teams giving the same number of
       balls to each side.

✦   Draw a circle on the ground and have one child from one team
       stand inside a circle, holding a bag/bucket. They cannot leave the
       circle.

✦   The rest of their team stands behind a line a short distance away,
       each of them holding a ball/beanbag.

✦   One player from the opposite team stands between the team
       and the child with the bag. This child will try to intercept the
       balls/bags and stop them reaching the player who has the bag.
       The object is to get as many of the balls as possible into the bag.

✦   The team with the most balls inside their bag at the end, wins.

22. **Balloon-basket** 8+

Co-operation/agility   **Equipment:** *Balloon for each pair, 8–10 hoops*

✦   Pair up the children and give each pair a balloon.

✦   For a class of about 30 pupils, place 12–15 hoops in a line on the ground, fairly well spaced out.

✦   Each pair must pass the balloon to each other as they make their way towards a hoop. (Each player is only allowed to pat the balloon twice in a row to keep it in the air before passing it to his/her partner.)

✦   To gain one point, one child from the pair must pick up a hoop and their partner must get the balloon to pass through it. They then move on to the next hoop.

✦   The children must try to gain as many points as they can by getting the balloon through as many hoops as possible. The winning pair is the one who manages to pass the balloon through the most hoops in the shortest length of time.

23. The king of the castle 8+

Speed/agility/co-operation **Equipment:** *Chalk, 2 x goal nets*

✦ Divide the children into two teams.

✦ Draw two large squares in front of two goal areas; these are the 'castles'.

✦ Stand two players from one team inside one castle, and two members from the other team in the other castle.

✦ Line up members of the opposing teams outside the castles. Each child has a ball to throw/roll through the castle and its defenders into the net behind.

✦ The players inside the castle will try to stop the balls getting inside. Any balls deflected or that don't get in can be retrieved and used again.

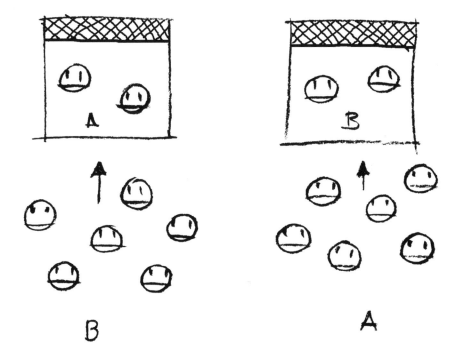

24. **Bursting balloons** 6+

Agility/speed   ***Equipment:*** *Balloons, string*

✦ This game needs to be played in a designated area.

✦ Pupils have a balloon tied to one of their ankles.

✦ The aim of the game is to step on and burst as many balloons as you can without getting your own burst.

✦ The child who manages to escape with their balloon unpopped wins.

25. **It's a 'push-over'!** 7+

Balance/agility   ***Equipment:*** *4 x PE mats*

✦ Place four PE mats into a square shape. Divide the children into pairs.

✦ Everyone gets hold of their right leg from behind with their right hand (so they end up with just their left leg on the floor).

✦ Using their left hand and shoulder, each child must try to make their partner lose balance.

Safety note: Children mustn't get too rough as they may fall on one another.

26. The 'waiters' race 7+

Balance/agility   **Equipment:** *2 x benches, 2 x plastic bottles, 2 x trays*

✦ This is a relay game. Divide each team in half and stand them facing each other at either ends of a bench. The first in each team will be holding a tray with a plastic bottle half full of water on it (with the lid on!).

✦ When the sign is given, the first member of the team walks along the bench to reach the other half of the team carrying the tray and the bottle. Then the tray and the bottle passes to the second member who will walk back along the bench and pass this onto the third member and so forth.

✦ If the bottle falls, or the person carrying it holds it to stop it falling, then that player will have to start from the end of the bench again.

✦ The first team to get all their players to go twice wins.

27. Ball knock-out! 8+

Aim/agility   ***Equipment:*** *1 x large soft ball, one tennis ball per child*

✦ Two teams stand facing each other a few metres apart. Each player must have a tennis ball. The teacher, in the middle, has a large soft ball.

✦ Once the teacher throws their ball into the air the pupils must try to hit it with their tennis balls. Pupils are only allowed to throw their balls when the teacher's ball is in the air.

✦ The team that hits the teacher's ball the most times wins.

Teaching PE Games

28. The hit

8+

Agility/aim/resistance

Equipment: *A small ball and hockey stick/golf club per child*

✦ The number of players must not be too large.

✦ Each player must have a small ball with a diameter of approximately 4cm and a hockey stick/golf club.

✦ On the playing area, make 10 holes approximately 10cm in diameter and not too deep (just enough to be able to hold the ball). Using the landscape available and adding obstacles, create two difficult holes, two easy, three of an average difficulty and two that are very difficult.

✦ The distance between the holes needs to be approximately 20m, and the holes made in areas with varying levels of difficulty.

✦ The winner is the child who completes the course in the least number of strokes.

29. **Lie down, stand up!** 7+

Agility/speed

✦ Divide the children into groups of five or six.

✦ The members of each team will form a line. Each member will pass their right hand between their legs to reach the left hand of the player behind them and the left hand will grab the right hand of the player in front.

✦ The group must then attempt to lie-down and get back up again without anybody letting go.

30. **Numbers** 7+

Agility/speed

✦ Groups run together around the game area. The teacher will call out a number and the groups have to arrange themselves into the shape of that number on the ground.

31. Burn out   6+

Agility/speed   **Equipment:** *Large soft balls*

✦   Two teams stand, one on each side of the field, with several balls
    for each team.

✦   When the game starts, the two teams throw balls at each other
    trying to hit an opposing team player. If the ball hits someone,
    that player becomes 'burnt' and will have to go to a specific spot
    behind the team that hit him. If the ball hits the floor first, then
    that player remains in play.

✦   Once players are 'burnt' they can rejoin their team if they
    manage to pick up a stray ball and hit a member of the
    opposition with it. (Balls can be thrown to the 'burnt' players, or
    can simply roll near them after being dodged.)

Variation: Players could have to do 10 star jumps (or some other
action) before rejoining the game.

32. **Break the chain**   7+

Resistance/agility

✦   This game involves groups of approximately eight players.

✦   Each group forms a line, holding each other's waist. The first member of each group moves along taking the rest of the group behind them, trying to make some of the players lose their grip.

✦   The one who lets go is out and the front person moves to the back. The new leader continues to make sudden movements in order to break the chain.

33. **Here comes the wolf!** 6+

Speed/agility/resistance/co-operation

✦ In groups of five, players hold each other's waists.

✦ Another player, the wolf, must try to touch the last person in the line.

✦ The first one in the line must lead the rest so that wolf can't catch the last player.

✦ The roles are exchanged either when the wolf catches the last person in the line or after an allotted time has passed.

34. **Shooting through hoops**   6+

Agility/co-operation/aim   **Equipment:** *Hoop, balls*

✦   Divide the class into teams.

✦   Each team stands in a line, 3m from a wall behind a marked throwing line.

✦   Lean a hoop against a wall. Team members take it in turns to throw a ball at the hoop. Every time a player manages to throw the ball inside the hoop, their team gains a point.

✦   The team that reaches a certain number of points wins.

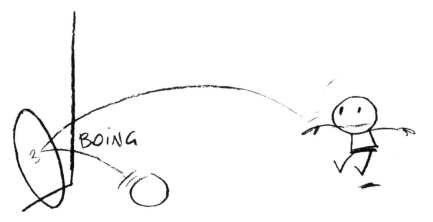

35. **Heads or catch**   6+

Agility/aim   **Equipment:** *Soft ball, brick wall*

✦   Line the children up one behind the other facing a wall.

✦   The first child has the ball and throws it high up against the wall and calls out either 'heads' or 'catch'. The second in line runs forward and has to either head the ball or catch it.

Variation: The children do the opposite of what has been said.

36. Catch it!   6+

Agility/reaction time   **Equipment:** *Soft balls*

✦ Two teams stand 5m apart. Each member from one team is given a ball. When the whistle is blown, the team with the balls must throw them into the air (to reach a certain height) and the other team must try to catch them before they reach the floor. Then the teams reverse roles.

✦ Let each team throw the balls into the air ten times.

✦ The team that catches the most balls wins.

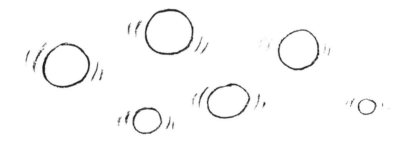

37. **Spinning tops** 6+

Balance/agility

✦ Mark out two parallel lines with a 10m distance between them. All the players must stand along one line.

✦ When the game starts, everybody runs towards the opposite line and back, spinning.

✦ Going to the line they will spin to their right and coming back they will spin to their left.

✦ The player that reaches the starting line first, wins.

38. **Bowling** 6+

Agility/aim   **Equipment:** *6 skittles and 3 balls per group*

✦ This game is played in groups. Each group has six skittles arranged to form a pentagon, with the sixth one in the centre. Players stand behind a line, approximately 3m away.

✦ Each player of each team uses the three balls to try to knock down the skittles. Players take it in turns to throw the balls, with the skittles being replaced for each player.

✦ One point is scored for each skittle knocked down, with a bonus point if they bowl down all six.

39. Throw the hoop   6+

Agility/aim   **Equipment:** *Bamboo canes, hoops*

✦ Push the bamboo sticks into the ground at different distances from a throwing line. Give each stick a set number of points.

✦ Players stand on a throwing line, one at a time. Each player will throw five hoops and try to get them on one of the sticks.

✦ The player with the most points, wins.

<u>Variation:</u> Try different-sized hoops and/or different heights of stick.

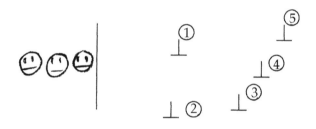

40. Hooping pegs 7+

Aim/agility   **Equipment:** *Coat rack or stand with three knobs or arms and six hoops per team*

✦   Divide the children into two teams and chalk a line approximately 4/5m away from a coatstand/coat rack.

✦   Each player will throw six hoops in the first round, aiming to get them on the hooks. Players should keep a written record of the scores.

✦   Play another two rounds and calculate each member's total points.

✦   If there is a draw/tie, there will be another round of hoop throwing, using the six hoops. The throwing line will be put back 1m.

✦   If a player manages to place all six hoops on the hooks/knobs then 10 points will be given. If all the six hoops are placed on the same hook/knob then 15 points will be awarded.

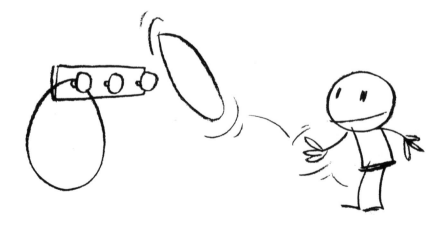

41. To clean the field 6+

Strength/agility/speed   **Equipment:** *Net and stand, hoops/discs*

✦   Two teams are separated by elastic or rope placed at a height of
     1.5–2m.

✦   The same number of hoops are placed on either side of the net.

✦   The game consists of the players throwing the hoops to the
     other side of the field, over the rope. If one of the hoops doesn't
     fall onto the other side, then they may pick it up again and have
     another go at throwing it over the rope to the opponents' side.

✦   The team that has the fewest hoops on their field after a set
     time wins.

✦   Opposing teams can pick up the hoops and throw them back.

1,5 - 2 m

42. **Score line** 6+

Agility/strength   **Equipment:** *Chalk, 3 x discuses per team*

✦   Three to four teams play with three discuses per player. Either play one team at a time or play with coloured discuses – one colour per team.

✦   The teams stand behind a line.

✦   In front of them there will be some areas marked on the floor with different values. The first member of each team throws their three discuses, trying to get them to land in one of the marked areas. If a discus falls on a line straddling two different areas, then no points are awarded. The points obtained by each of the players are added up for the team; the team with the most points win.

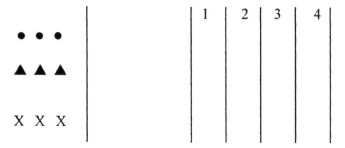

43. Your turn

8+

Agility/time of reaction   **Equipment:** *Tennis balls*

✦   This is played in teams of five. Each player in a team is given a number and each team has a tennis ball.

✦   The first player throws their ball against the wall and calls out a number, that player must then run forward and catch the ball before it hits the ground and then quickly throw it against the wall calling out another number.

✦   If the ball hits the floor, that player loses a life. When three lives are lost then that player is out.

Variation: Try using different types of ball, eg volleyball, soft foam ball, etc. Larger balls will be slower.

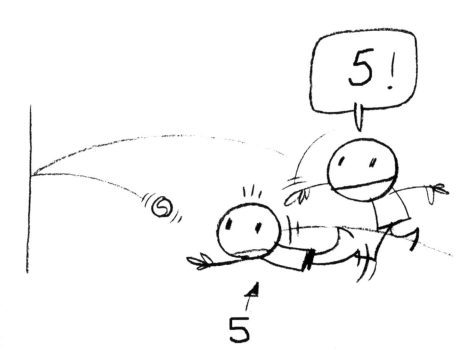

44. Net score   8+

Agility/aim   *Equipment: Chalk, netball goal, ball*

✦   This is played on a basketball/netball court. Draw three
    semicircular lines 3, 4 and 5m away from the net. Write down
    in each section the number of points the children will receive if
    they score: 10, 15 and 20 respectively, from the inner circle going
    out.

✦   Each player throws a ball three times, one from each of the set
    distances: one from the inner, one from the middle and then one
    from the outside.

✦   Each time a player scores, points are awarded according to the
    section the player is standing in.

✦   The player who accumulates the most points wins.

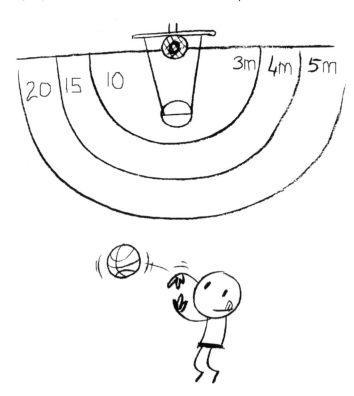

Chapter 3
Resistance games

Resistance is the human body's capacity to sustain a physical activity or effort for as long as possible, fighting off fatigue.

Physical activities can be divided into two types:

- *Aerobic or organic*: medium or low intensity activities. The oxygen which reaches the muscles is needed to help sustain the effort for a prolonged period. The work is low intensity/long duration.

- *Anaerobic or muscular*: high intensity activities. The oxygen reaching the muscles is insufficient and produces a need for more. The work is high intensity/short duration.

Resistance improves how well our heart, respiratory system and muscles work. It's a source of energy. In our early years it evolves gradually as we grow. From age 7–8 it has a moderate progression.

45. **The first passes** 7+

Time of reaction (speed)/co-ordination   **Equipment:** *Whistle*

✦ Split the class into groups of about ten players each. Each group gets into a line, one player behind the other along a running track.

✦ Each group jogs slowly around the track. When the teacher blows a whistle they increase their speed, still keeping in line.

✦ Now each time the whistle sounds the last member of the line runs faster to overtake the group and be first in the line.

✦ This exercise is repeated until everybody in the group has had a chance to overtake.

✦ If anyone in the group isn't capable of completing this task and cannot overtake the whole group, they will be out.

46. **Cops and robbers** 7+

Speed/agility   **Equipment:** *Squares of paper with the letter C, sticky tape*

✦ Choose two players to start as cops; the others are all robbers. The cops must chase and catch the robbers.

✦ Each cop has a 'C' written on paper and stuck to him/her.

✦ When a cop catches a robber, the robber then becomes a cop and sticks a 'C' on himself/herself.

✦ Continue until all the robbers have been caught. The last remaining robber is the winner.

47. Who do we catch? 7+

Speed/agility **Equipment:** *Ball*

✦ All players are spread out on the playing field.

✦ One child is given charge of the ball and his/her aim is to keep the ball as long as possible while the other children try to take it from him/her. When he/she sees he/she might get caught, he/she can throw the ball to another pupil who will try to catch it and run away, once again chased by everyone else including the player who has just thrown the ball.

✦ If a player catches the child with the ball then it's his/her turn to hold the ball and run away from everybody else.

48. **Swing-ball** 6+

Co-ordination/speed   ***Equipment:*** *Soft ball, net-fruit bag, short length of rope*

✦   Everyone stands in a circle with one child in the middle of the circle with a ball tied onto a rope.

✦   Use a soft ball to prevent injury and place it in a 'fruit-net-bag' and tie a rope to the end.

✦   The player swings the rope around within the circle, just above the floor, and the children in the circle must jump over it. (Make sure the player in the middle passes the rope from hand to hand, rather than spinning round and round, so they don't get too dizzy!)

✦   Anyone that does not jump over the ball or is hit by it must take the position in the centre and swing the ball around.

49. Jump the rope   8+

Strength/co-ordination   ***Equipment:*** *Length of rope (approx 4m)*

✦   The game must be played in an area of about 20m x 4m – the 'pitch'.

✦   All the players, except two, must be inside the pitch. The other two hold either end of a rope, approx 30cm above the ground. These two children must then walk from one end of the pitch to the other.

✦   All of the other children in the pitch must jump over the rope or else get eliminated.

✦   The height of the rope can be increased when there are fewer players in the field, in order to eliminate children slowly.

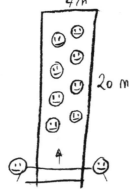

50. Skipping game 7+

Co-ordination/agility/strength **Equipment:** *Skipping rope*

✦ Divide the class into groups of five.

✦ Two players hold a long skipping rope. They must move the rope (by turning it over and over or swinging it from side to side) so that the other three players can jump in.

✦ The players jump in one at a time and continue jumping while the other players join in jumping, until all three players are jumping.

✦ The one that causes the rope to stop takes a turn holding the rope.

51. Catch the fleet 8+

Speed/agility **Equipment:** *Enough balls per child*

✦ The number of balls used in this game must be equal to the number of players minus one.

✦ The balls are spread out over the field. The players must run about the field and, when the teacher blows the whistle, the children must try to pick up a ball. The one that does not get a ball gains a point.

✦ Spread the balls out again and repeat as before. The one that has fewest points, wins.

52. **Don't jump!**   8+

Strength/speed/co-ordination   **Equipment:** *Lengths of rope*

✦   This game is played in pairs, apart from one player who stays alone. Each pair has a rope which they hold by the end; it must be loose and dangle between them.

✦   All the pairs run around keeping the ropes loose. The single player must try and jump over the ropes and the pairs must avoid this happening by running away.

✦   When the player manages to jump over a rope then that pair must put down the rope and start trying to jump over other ropes too.

✦   The last remaining pair win.

Safety Note: It is important that the ropes are not so high that the runners trip up. You could say that if you see a rope higher than 20cm (or whatever height you set), that pair will have to set down their rope and become runners.

53. Collectors   8+

Strength   **Equipment:** *Balls, whistle*

✦   Divide the children into four equal teams, one team in each
        corner of the field.

✦   Place some balls in the centre of the playing area. (There should
        be fewer balls in the centre than players.)

✦   Tell the children that when the signal is given, everyone
        should race towards the centre. At your command they change
        between: jumping feet together, skipping, hopping on one foot,
        squat jumping, etc.

✦   Each player can only take one ball. The team that manages to
        gather the most balls and take them to their corner wins.

✦   Afterwards, the balls are put back in the centre and the game is
        played all over again. A point is given to the team that wins each
        game.

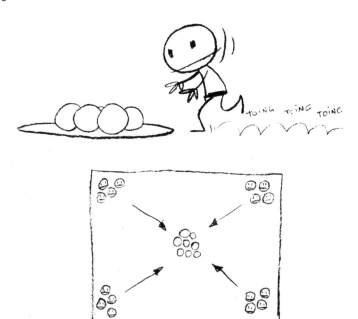

54. **Jumpers** 8+

Strength/co-ordination **Equipment:** *1 hoop*

✦ All the players jump about the field, with their feet held close together.

✦ Choose a single player and give him/her a hoop to carry. His/her aim is to jump after the other childen and attempt to catch them with the hoop.

✦ When a jumper is caught, the children can either swap roles or he/she can become an additional catcher.

55. **Blow up balloons** 7+

Strength **Equipment:** *Balloons, bucket, balloon pump*

✦ This activity is played in teams. Each team needs a bucket or bag to put balloons in.

✦ Each pupil must complete a designated activity circuit, then once the circuit has been completed blow up a balloon with the pump and put it in the sack. The second member of the team can't start their circuit until the first one has put the blown up balloon in the sack. (Getting the balloon could be part of the course.)

56. Hop it   8+

Strength/co-ordination/balance

✦ Divide the children into pairs and number them either one or two.

✦ Players run around individually. When their number is called they must chase their partner, both hopping on one leg (for an 8–10 second duration.)

✦ After this period, children continue running about and the other number will be called out.

✦ Each time someone catches his or her partner, a point is awarded.

57. **Frog fight** 8+

Balance/strength

✦ Divide the class into two teams and mark out two parallel lines with a distance of 5m between them.

✦ The teams crouch like frogs behind each line. When the signal is given, they jump towards one another. The aim is to tag a player from the other team by placing a hand on his/her shoulder. This 'kills' the frog who should then stand up.

✦ When the next signal is given, the players that remain crouching return to their places behind the line and any players that were standing are out.

✦ Repeat until one team wins.

58. Jump through hoops   8+

Agility/strength   **Equipment:** *Hoops*

✦   Divide the children into two equal teams.

✦   Sit one team down in a circle with enough space between
    players for each to hold one side of a hoop at shoulder level.

✦   The other team must go around the circle, jumping through each
    hoop (from outside the circle to the inside and from inside to
    outside, like in a zig-zag.)

✦   Afterwards, the teams swap over.

✦   The team that is the quickest at this, wins.

59. **What a parcel!**   **8+**

Speed

✦   In pairs, form two concentric circles, the pairs must face each other.

✦   Two players are 'free' and one must start chasing the other one around the outside of the circles.

✦   In order not to get caught, the one being chased must pass between the circle pairs and stand in front of someone within the inner circle (in front of a parcel). The player who is the partner of the parcel now starts chasing the original chaser in the opposite direction.

✦   If any one is caught, then the roles are exchanged.

60. Transported in style! 10+

Strength   *Equipment: 1 mat for each team*

✦   Divide the class into teams of five.

✦   Set out designated routes with four stopping points at regular intervals for each team.

✦   One of the players lies down on a mat.

✦   The other four players must hold on to the corners of the mat and carry the other member. At every stopping point along the route, the team must swap so a new player is being carried on the mat.

✦   The team that finishes the whole route first, wins.

61. **Paper round!** 8+

Speed   **Equipment:** *A newspaper*

✦ Everyone, except one, stands in a circle facing inwards with their hands behind their back.

✦ The remaining player must carry a rolled up newspaper, or something similar, and go around the other players.

✦ As he/she passes a child of their choice, he/she leaves the newspaper in the player's hands and swaps places with them.

✦ The one that receives the newspaper must go round the circle once and then choose someone else by touching them on the shoulder with the newspaper. Then he/she will run around the outside circle and try to fill the other's place without being caught.

✦ If the child with the newspaper makes it round without being caught, they swap over roles.

Chapter 4
Speed games

Speed is the capacity to complete motor actions, one or more movements, in the shortest time possible.

Speed enhances the functioning of the nervous and muscular systems. It increases our capacity for extension and flexibility and improves muscle tone.

It develops in conjunction with co-ordination and strength.

8 to 10 years is a good age to start developing speed.

Speed allows for greater co-ordination and concentration.

We could say there are four types of speed: reactive, explosive, progressive and sustained.

62. **Tagged!** 8+

Co-ordination/agility

✦ Divide the class into two teams, A and B.

✦ Teams A and B stand at opposite ends of the playing area. Team A players hold out a hand, palm facing upwards.

✦ A player from team B runs over to team A and chooses a player to tag by touching his/her palm. The team B player then runs back to their team as fast as they can, pursued by the member of team A who has just been tagged.

✦ If player B isn't caught then the process is repeated, by another member of team B.

✦ If player B is caught, he/she has to stand with team A and when a member from team B comes to tag someone, the two team B players will hold hands and run back together to the safety of their own zone.

✦ If both of them are caught, both must return to team A, and wait until another player from team B comes to their rescue. If they all manage to hold hands and reach their team base without being caught then they are all saved and can once again rejoin their team.

63. **Heads and tails** 6+

Agility/resistance

✦ This game is best played on a marked out court or pitch with two baselines and a central line.

✦ Players form two rows, one each side of the central line. Each row is a team: 'heads' and 'tails'.

✦ Ask one child volunteer to be 'Mother', and to stand with his/her back to everyone and call out orders. If the 'mother' calls 'heads', all the players of this team must try to catch a player from the 'tails' team who should try to escape to their baseline (which represents home).

✦ 'Mother' can change her mind when she likes. For each player caught, one point is awarded.

64. **Four corners** 6+

Resistance

✦ All players run in a circle in the centre of the court.

✦ When the teacher shouts 'Go', the children run to a corner. The last one to reach a corner is eliminated and the rest will go back to the centre and continue playing.

✦ If only one player goes to a particular corner he/she is not eliminated.

✦ When only a few players are left, start to remove certain corners.

65. The lottery ticket 8+

Strength/agility **Equipment:** *Chalk, soft ball, pen and paper*

✦ Play in teams of approximately ten players.

✦ Draw a circle, with a diameter of about 10m and place a large soft ball in the centre. The players stand around the outside.

✦ Make a table with six columns. In the first column write the names of the football teams each player wants to represent. Leave the remaining columns blank for recording scores. The teacher calls out the name of a football team and throws the ball into the centre of the circle. The child who chose that team quickly runs to get the ball.

✦ Once a player has picked up the ball, they must throw the ball at one of the other 'football teams' that form the circle.

✦ If the ball hits the child, then a tick is given to the thrower's team. However, if the thrower misses, then a tick is given to that player's team.

✦ The winner is the first one to get five ticks along his/her line.

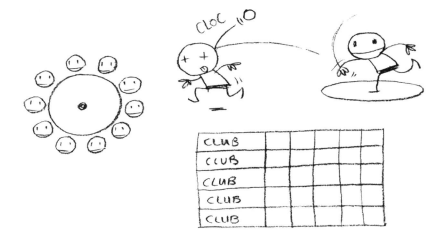

66. **Fetch the ball** 7+

Agility/resistance (if played several times)   **Equipment:** *Balls and hoops as per children in one team*

✦   Divide the class into two equal teams.

✦   Each team stands behind the start line, facing one another.

✦   In between the teams there are as many hoops as there are players on one team. Inside each hoop is a ball. The players on each team must choose a hoop and line themselves up opposite it.

✦   When the teacher signals, both sets of team players run toward their chosen hoop and aim to get to the ball before their opponent.

✦   The players that return to the start line with the ball gain a point for their team.

67. **Mixed-up fields** 7+

Co-operation/collaboration/co-ordination/agility   **Equipment:** *1 ball*

✦   This game involves two teams and one ball.

✦   The ball mustn't bounce, players can't take more than three steps while holding the ball, and the ball can't be held for longer than 10 seconds.

✦   The game consists of passing the ball between team members without members of the other team catching it. When the other team catches the ball, then it is their turn to pass it to each other.

✦   The team that does not have the ball has to intercept the passes of the other team in order to get the ball back.

Variation: More balls can be introduced into the game.

68. **Through the tunnel** 7+

Resistance/agility   **Equipment:** *Whistle*

✦   Divide the class into pairs. The pairs then place themselves in a circle one behind the other forming two concentric circles.

✦   The players that are on the inside stand with their legs apart.

✦   When the teacher blows the whistle, the players on the outside start running clockwise around the circle. On the teacher's second whistle, they must carry on until reaching their partner and crawl between their legs and stand up in front of them.

✦   The last one to do so, is penalized with a point.

✦   Swap over roles.

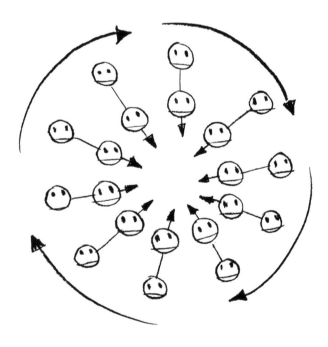

69. The pot   7+

Co-ordination/agility/resistance

◆   Three or four players hold hands and chase the other players.

◆   They catch other players by encircling and trapping them. The caught player then joins them by holding hands with the others and chasing the players who are still running around freely.

◆   The space in which this game is played should be limited.

70. The fugitive letter   6+

Agility/co-ordination

◆   This activity is played in groups of three. The players A, B and C start moving very closely together.

◆   When the teacher calls out one of these three letters, this player must escape from the other two who must try to catch him/her.

◆   After about a minute the game is stopped. If the player has not been caught, he/she gains a point. If he/she has been caught, then the other players get the point.

◆   Continue until all the letters have been called several times.

71. **Dodgeball** 6+

Agility　　　**Equipment:** *As many balls as players*

✦ Divide children into two teams.

✦ In between both teams is a common area where there are as many balls as players on one team.

✦ Teams take it in turns to pick up the balls and throw them at the other team, who try to dodge the balls. For safety reasons, balls should be below shoulder height.

✦ The players who get hit are out. Each player can only throw one ball. Time the teams to find which team managed to get their opposition members out first.

72. **Touch the colour** 6+

Agility/reflexes

✦ The children run around a designated area.

✦ The teacher calls out a colour. The players must then run as fast as possible to touch something of that specific colour.

73. **The wheels** 6+

Agility

✦ One person from each pair forms an inner circle. The other children form an outer circle, lining up opposite their partner leaving a gap of approximately 1m between circles.

✦ The circles walk round in opposite directions. When the sign is given, the players in the inner circle must try to tag their partner, who will try to escape.

✦ Before starting, specify the playing area.

✦ After 10 seconds stop the game, and players swap roles.

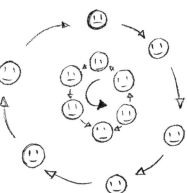

74. **The fox and the chickens** 6+

Resistance/agility   **Equipment:** *As many scarves as children*

✦ Choose one player to be the fox. The rest of the players are chickens and must tuck a scarf into their belts or waistbands as if it were a tail.

✦ The fox must try to catch one of the children's tails and put it on him/herself. Whoever loses his/her tail turns into the fox.

75. **Change the colour** 6+

Resistance/agility   ***Equipment:*** *Balls of different colours, hoops*

✦   This is a relay race. Two teams line up behind the start. The first player has a ball.

✦   At set distances from the starting line, set up several hoops for each team, each with a ball inside.

✦   When the signal is given, the first player of each team runs with the ball to the first hoop. He/she changes the ball for the one inside the first hoop, runs to the secong hoop and swaps the ball with the one in the second hoop. The second ball is put in the third hoop and so on until the ball in the last hoop has been swapped.

✦   The player then runs back to the start line with the ball from the last hoop and gives it to the next player in line who then does the same.

✦   The team that finishes first, wins.

     Teaching PE Games

76. Pursuit of four   8+

Resistance/co-ordination

✦   Four teams are needed. Make a square using all the players, each team forming one side. Each player must place themselves in numeric order, starting with number 1.

✦   The teacher calls out a number and the players from each team with that number start running outside the square to the right, chasing the player in front of him/herself and trying not to get caught at the same time.

✦   Whoever tags another player gains a point, but must not forget to let go quickly as another player may well be coming from behind to catch him/her. The team with the most points wins.

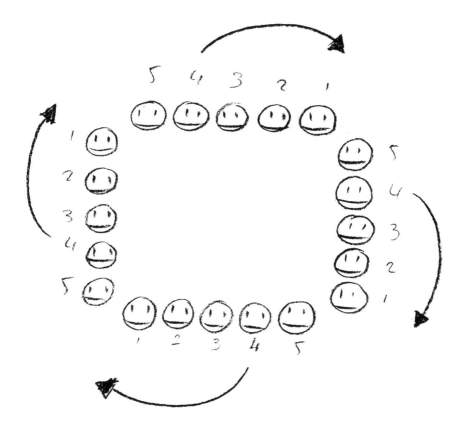

77. **Star chase**

Resistance/agility

✦   Divide the children into groups of six. The groups make lines fanning out from the centre to form a star. Choose one player from one group to start.

✦   The child starting must go around the star, jogging, and when passing a child forming the end arm of the star must say 'come with me' or 'go out the other side'. The child this has been said to must either race against the first child in the same direction or race in the opposite direction to get back to his/her position in the 'star'.

✦   The last child to arrive is the one to start the next round, and the other player rejoins his/her group but at the middle of the star.

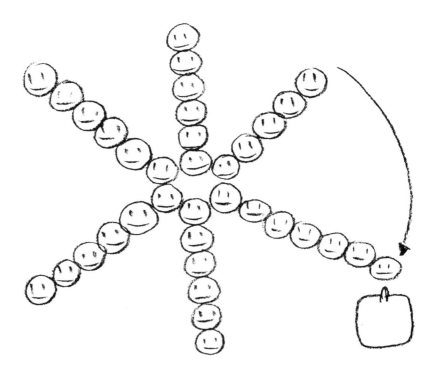

78. **Ball and hoop relay**   6+

Agility/co-ordination   ***Equipment:*** *Hoops and balls (or beanbags)*

✦   All teams must form a line behind the starting line. Next to each team there is a hoop with three balls inside.

✦   Place three more hoops per team, at set distances from the line.

✦   When the signal is given, the first team member runs out with a ball that he/she has taken from their team's hoop. The player places the ball in the first hoop and then runs back for another ball, placing it in the second hoop and then runs back again to collect the last ball and place it in the third hoop.

✦   The player runs back to the team and touches the hand of the player next in line. This player runs and brings all the balls back to the initial hoop, one at a time.

✦   The third member puts the balls in the hoop as the first did, etc.

Variation: This game can also be played with beanbags.

79. **Throw and catch volleyball** 7+

Agility/co-ordination   **Equipment:** *Rope/net, as many balls as players*

✦   Divide the class into teams of three or four players. Each player will need a ball.

✦   Place a rope/net about 2m high. Play two teams at a time. Both teams stand in a row on the same side of the rope/net and at a specific distance from it. The first member of each team throws the ball over the rope/net and must run to catch it on the other side, before it touches the floor. The second player does the same, and so on.

✦   Each time the ball touches the floor, a point is given to the opposite team. The team with the most points win. Swap teams so everyone has a go.

80. **Wolves and lambs** 7+

Resistance

✦ Four players are the wolves and the rest are lambs. Players spread out over a playing field. The wolves each control their own corner of the field.

✦ When the teacher gives a signal, the wolves try to catch the lambs. Each lamb that is caught by a wolf will be taken to that wolf's corner. The wolf that catches the most lambs, wins.

✦ Exchange roles and repeat the game.

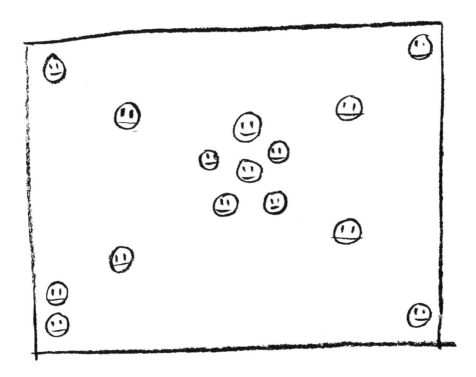

81. The cell 7+

Co-ordination/agility   **Equipment:** *A hoop*

✦ Players spread out across the playing field except for two, who stay and form a pair by holding each other's hands.

✦ This pair then try to catch and take the rest of the players to their cell (a hoop).

✦ Any player taken to the cell must wait until another player is captured and then they can form a new pair and become chasers too.

82. Ball recall! 6+

Agility   **Equipment:** *1 ball*

✦ Give each player a number. All the players should stand in a circle.

✦ One player goes in the centre of the circle holding a ball. He/she says a number out loud and throws the ball into the air; the player with that number must try to catch the ball before it falls on the floor or he/she will be eliminated.

✦ The player catching the ball is the new thrower.

83. **Everybody catch** 6+

Resistance/co-ordination

✦ Divide the class into teams of five. In each team number the children from 1–5.

✦ The teacher calls out one of the numbers. Each team runs after their team player whose number has just been called out.

✦ When this person is caught, the teacher calls out another number and the team goes after the person with that number.

✦ Points are awarded to those who catch the player or the player who is not caught after a given time.

✦ You will need to clearly define the playing area.

84. **Balls out** 7+

Strength/agility   **Equipment:** *Net, 2 boxes of balls*

✦ Two teams stand on opposite sides of a net placed in the middle of a court. Set a time limit for the game.

✦ A box of balls is placed at either end of the court, one for each team.

✦ On the sound of a whistle, children from both teams pick up and throw the balls down the court and over the net towards the opposing team.

✦ Both teams must prevent any ball dropping or bouncing on their end of the court. Players can either punch the balls out of their court area or back over the net to the opposition. They are not, however, allowed to get any closer than 3m to the net before throwing the ball over.

✦ When the time period has elapsed, the team that has the least balls left on their side of the court wins.

85. **Drawing relay**   6+

Co-ordination   **Equipment:** *Easel, paper, coloured crayons and pencils/chalks*

✦   Decide on a subject for the drawing. This example is a landscape, but instead you could choose an image related to a current topic.

✦   Teams stand in a line behind each other at the starting line. 20m from the starting line is a drawing board per team.

✦   The first member of each group runs up to the board with a crayon/pencil and draws a certain element of the scenery! He/she then runs back and passes the crayon/pencil to the second player and he does the same, drawing another item and so on until everybody in the team has had a go.

✦   Allocate points to the fastest team and for the best picture. The team with the most points, wins.

86. **Leapfrog chase** 6+

Strength/resistance/agility

◆ Choose a number of children to be chasers and runners.

◆ Everybody else must be scattered around the playing field, in a crouched position.

◆ The chasers must try to catch the runners. When a runner hops over someone that is crouched, then they must swap places and the other player turns into a runner.

◆ If a chaser touches a runner, their roles must change.

◆ The number of chasers and runners can be increased.

Teaching PE Games

87. **Give me your hand** 6+

Agility/ resistance

✦ All the players run around the playing field in pairs, holding hands.

✦ One player is left free.

✦ This free player must try to get hold of the hand of one of the paired-up players. When a paired player is caught he/she must let go of their original partner's hand. This player is now left free and must find a new partner.

88. **Swat the fly** 6+

Agility/resistance   **Equipment:** *1 foam baton*

✦ Choose one child to be the 'swatter' and the rest will be 'flies'.

✦ The swatter chases the flies and tries to swat them using the foam baton. Any children swatted are out.

89. **Colours**   6+

Agility/speed

✦   Sit the children down in a circle.

✦   Identify each player by using colours: green, blue, yellow and red, repeating this order until everyone has a colour.

✦   Give orders, such as 'Blues to the right' they will run around the circle, to their right, until all the 'Blue' players have reached their place in the circle.

✦   For 'Reds to the left' the same is done but this time to the left.

✦   The last person to sit down gains a point.

✦   The aim is to gain the least points. The child with the fewest points at the end wins.

Chapter 5
Strength Games

Strength is the ability to exert muscular force against internal or external resistance, in order to set off or oppose a static or moving mass/form.

Force is an action or an influence capable of modifying the state of a moving or static body, and accelerating or modifying its speed.

Strength improves the work done by our bones, joints and muscles. It develops muscular mass, the physical domain and postural tone; it improves our muscular metabolism and co-ordination.

There are different types of strength:
- Dynamic or isotonic strength: the part involved moves or changes position.

- Static or isometric: the part involved remains stationary.

- Explosive: sudden mobilization.

90. **Worm race** 7+

Resistance

✦ Various ropes are tied to wall bars.

✦ The players, lying on the floor, must reach the wall using only the ropes and their arms to pull themselves along.

✦ You can hold elimination rounds, with the winners competing in a final.

91. Guard your line   8+

Balance/agility

✦ Mark out two paths, 20m long and 10cm wide, and 60cm apart.

✦ Divide the children into pairs. One player walks along one path and the other player walks along the other. The players must try to unbalance their opponent, by pushing them.

✦ Whenever a player steps outside the line of the path they are out.

✦ The winners must play against each other until there is only one winner left.

Safety note: Remind the children not to push an opponent too hard. Point out that pushng too hard might cause them to step outside the path themselves.

92. Basket!

9+

Resistance/agility/co-ordination   **Equipment:** *6 hoops, 5 heavy balls*

✦   Scatter six hoops around the playing field.

✦   The players must stand at a certain distance from the hoops behind a line.

✦   The further a hoop is from the line, the greater the value.

✦   Each player throws five balls trying to get them to land in the hoops. The heavier the balls, the harder this will be. Balls weighing 2kg work well.

✦   The points that each player gets are added up and the player with most points wins.

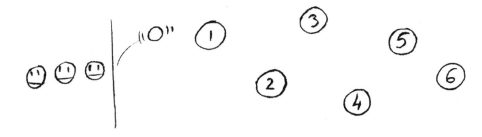

93. Bull's-eye shotput 9+

Co-ordination/resistance   ***Equipment:*** *1 heavy ball per team*

✦   This activity requires teams lined up and standing a few metres away from a wall.

✦   Each team will have a ball weighing about 2kg.

✦   Draw three targets on the wall for each team, allocating a certain number of points for each according to height and size.

✦   The first player in each team stands with his/her back towards the wall like a shotputter, in front of the targets. He/she must turn and throw the ball trying to hit the targets. Allow three throws per child quickly in succession.

✦   The second player will do the same as the first and so on, until everyone has had a turn. The points achieved by all the players in each team are added up.

✦   The team with most points wins.

94. **Piggyback guides** 10+

Resistance/co-ordination ***Equipment:*** *Items to create obstacle course*

✦ In pairs, one child climbs on the other's back for a 'piggy-back' ride. The person doing the carrying, is blindfolded.

✦ The player who can see must guide the other around an obstacle track by giving directions.

✦ The pair that finishes first wins.

Safety note: Make sure that the pairs are equally matched. Tell the children that they can swap positions if it gets too tiring.

95. Hopping pairs 10+

Resistance/balance/co-ordination

✦ Divide the children into pairs and give each child in the pair a number, 1 or 2.

✦ All of the players run around. When a number is called out, players with that number must chase their partner for 10 seconds. Both of them must do so hopping on one foot.

✦ If a player catches their partner, they swap roles and the one who was caught becomes the chaser.

✦ Afterwards the other number is called out and the game continues.

96. **The frogs and the acrobats** 7+

Resistance/balance/co-ordination

✦ The playing area must be well specified from the beginning.

✦ The players who are 'acrobats' move around on one foot only. (If they ever use both feet they will be eliminated.)

✦ The 'frog' players must chase the acrobats by crouching and then jumping around on all fours. The 'acrobats' who are caught are eliminated.

<u>Variation:</u> Any 'acrobats' who are caught by a 'frog' turn into 'frogs'.

97. On horseback!   11+

Co-ordination/resistance   ***Equipment:*** *Balls*

✦   There are four players in each team, which will be two pairs made by a 'rider' and a 'horse'. The 'rider' rides on the back of the 'horse'.

✦   The riders of one team pass each other the ball, without it falling. The opposite team tries to catch the ball.

✦   If the other team manages to get the ball then they start passing between each other.

✦   Swap roles.

98. Medieval tournament   11+

Co-ordination/agility/resistance/balance

✦   This is played in pairs, with one player 'riding' (as if a horse) on the other player's back.

✦   They will try to unbalance the other riders.

✦   Last pair standing wins.

99. The scarf knight 11+

Resistance ***Equipment:*** *Scarf or ribbon*

✦ Equal numbers of players stand in two concentric circles.

✦ When the signal is given, the players on the exterior circle get on the backs of the players in the inner circle. (Match children up carefully.)

✦ One of the 'riders' has a scarf or a ribbon tied to his waist and runs away galloping. When the second signal is given, the rest of the knights and their 'horses' must chase after him and try to snatch the ribbon/scarf.

✦ The 'riders' and 'horses' keep on swapping roles. The one that manages to catch the ribbon/scarf wears it in the next game.

100. The horses in a circle 11+

Speed/agility/co-ordination **Equipment:** *Beanbags (or other objects)*

✦ Equal numbers of players stand in two concentric circles. Place some objects, eg beanbags, inside the inner circle, one less than the number of pairs.

✦ When the signal is given, the players on the exterior circle walk around the whole circle once. Then they crawl between their partner's legs and end up in the middle of the circle where they will pick up one of the objects.

✦ The last one ends up without an object and is given a point.

✦ The roles are swapped at the end of each round.

✦ The pair with the fewest points at the end of the game wins.

Chapter 6
Winding-down games

After any physical activity we need to return to our natural state, letting the tension, tiredness and stress of the physical exercise go, little by little.

Relaxation produces a state where mind and body are in complete harmony. We aim to achieve a feeling of peace and well-being after exercises of a certain intensity.

Relaxation comes to us through concentration and psychological rest. It reduces anxiety and irritability. It helps our breathing (which oxygenates better when our muscles are relaxed) and our cardiovascular system returns to the naturally calm and even functioning state. This in turn enhances muscular relaxation.

Stress can accelerate the ageing process; every minute spent in relaxation is equivalent to an extra day of life.

Teaching PE Games

101. The boat 6+

Paying attention/concentration/memory

✦ Sit the children down in a circle.

✦ Explain that one player starts by saying: 'A boat has just sailed from overseas full of ... ', and he/she gives the name of an animal etc.

✦ One by one, everyone in the circle must repeat the sentence, saying the word(s) that have been said already (in this case an animal) and add their own.

✦ Children must not spend a lot of time thinking about it.

Variations: The game can also be played using words that begin with a specific letter. Alternatively players could be forbidden from repeating a word that has already been used.

102. Crazy questions   6+

Attention/memory

✦   Everyone sits down in a circle.

✦   One child starts by whispering a question into the ear of the
    child sitting next to him/her. That child then whispers back an
    answer to the question. The second child whispers a question
    to the third player and this child then answers them back. Then
    the third player asks a question to the fourth one and so on until
    everyone has asked and answered someone else's question.

✦   When all of the players in the circle have both asked and
    answered a question, the children must then take it in turns to
    repeat what they had heard.
    - _____ asked me (and then they say what that player
      had asked them)
    - _____ answered (and then they say what that player
      had answered).

103. **The blind hen** 6+

Socialization/memory **Equipment:** *Blindfold*

✦ Stand the children in a circle holding hands.

✦ Choose a child to become the 'hen', who will be placed in the centre of the circle, blindfolded. The players sing, 'Blind hen, what did you lose?' The hen answers back, 'a thimble and a needle'. To which the children in the circle answer, 'turn three times and you will find them.'

✦ The hen is turned three times and tries to find someone from the circle. When the hen has found a player, the hen must then guess who it is. If the guess is correct then this person will be the next hen; if the guess is incorrect then the one playing the hen carries on.

104. Catch the thief! 6+

Co-ordination/concentration

✦ Choose one child to be the 'detective', and ask the other children to sit in a circle.

✦ Without letting the detective know, choose another child from the circle to act as the 'thief'. The thief starts to wink at the other members within the circle, trying to conceal his/her identity from the detective.

✦ The children that are winked at must say 'jail'. Meanwhile, the detective is scouting the perimeter of the circle trying to discover who the thief is. If the thief is discovered, then he/she must swap with the detective and another thief is chosen.

✦ Play continues for a selected time period. If the thief is not discovered then award him/her ten points and choose another detective and thief.

105. Hot ball 6+

Speed/co-ordination/agility **Equipment:** *Ball*

✦ Children stand in a circle. They must pass a ball to the person on their right as quickly as possible without dropping it.

✦ When the teacher blows the whistle, the one that has the ball is out.

106. The 'backboard' 6+

Co-ordination/concentration

✦ In pairs, one player tilts forward (leaving their back parallel as though he/she is a table) and the other player writes a word using their finger on the first player's back.

✦ The one that is positioned as a table must guess what the word is. The game gets more complicated when the words are longer or by using short sentences.

✦ After a while swap over roles.

107. The jumper   6+

Agility/co-ordination/speed   **Equipment:** *ball*

✦ Divide children into pairs.

✦ One member of the pair throws the ball up against the wall at knee height for his/her partner to jump over it when it bounces. The 'thrower' then has to catch the ball.

✦ Each time a member misses jumping over the ball or hits the ball accidently he/she gains a point.

✦ Repeat 6–10 times and swap over. The pair with the fewest points at the end wins.

108. Human noughts and crosses   6+

Agility/co-ordination/co-operation   ***Equipment:*** *9 hoops*

✦   This game requires nine hoops and two teams with three players each. Place the hoops on the ground in a 3 x 3 square.

✦   The aim of the game is for one of the teams to form a straight line using all three of its players, before the other team does.

✦   The team that manages to do so first will win.

✦   Flip a coin to decide which team begins. Teams take it in turns to move. Each player must place themselves in a hoop, to form 'three in a row'.

109. **Fumbling around!**   6+

Co-operation/agility/concentration   ***Equipment:*** *2 x blindfolds, plastic object, table (optional)*

✦   Two teams stand facing each other – there shouldn't be much distance between both teams. Give each team member a specific number. Use the same numbers for both teams.

✦   In the middle, between both of the teams, place a plastic object either on the floor or on a small table.

✦   When the teacher calls out a number, the two players (from opposite teams) with the same number should be blindfolded. They must then walk/crawl towards the object and see which of them will get to it first.

✦   The other members from their team are allowed to give directions, but the blindfolded child must concentrate hard on what they hear as there will be two teams shouting commands. The one that reaches the object first will gain a point for their team.

110. Woof, woof!   6+

Co-ordination/agility

✦   Children sit down in a circle.

✦   The children number themselves in order, from 1 to 6, in
    a whisper. Any player can start, with play continuing in a
    clockwise direction.

✦   The child who would normally be given the number 7 has to say
    out loud 'woof, woof'.

✦   If this person gets it wrong, and does not say 'woof, woof', he/
    she is out. If it is said properly, then the game will continue but
    with a different player starting.

Variation: You can play the game using two numbers in a set
sequence, or by counting to 100 but every time the number 7 comes
up, the child has to say 'Woof, woof', ie 7, 17 ,27, 37 etc.

111. **Sending messages** 6+

Agility/co-ordination

✦   Everyone sits down in a circle holding hands and one child sits in the centre of the circle.

✦   One of the children in the circle says 'I send a message to ...' (name a player within the circle) and he/she gently squeezes the hand of his/her neighbour and the neighbour will press the hand of the next person and so on until the message is passed down to the person it is directed to. When the hand of the person the message is directed to is pressed then he/she must say out loud 'it has arrived'.

✦   The child in the middle of the circle has to find out which direction the message is being sent. His/her aim is to stop the message before it reaches the intended recipient. If the child manages to find out in time, he/she wins and the one that sent the message must go into the middle! If he/she doesn't find out in time and the message reaches the intended person then he/she will stay in the middle of the circle.

112. Fruit mix-up 6+

Velocity/agility **Equipment:** *1 hoop per child*

✦ Place the hoops in a circle. One pupil sits in the centre of the circle and all other players sit within a hoop.

✦ The pupils are identified using fruits: apple, orange and pear, until everybody in the group has been given one of the three names.

✦ The pupil in the middle is a lemon.

✦ When the teacher calls out a fruit, eg 'apple', then all the apples must stand up, go around the circle and sit down in a hoop that belonged to another apple; the lemon must also try to sit down in one of those 'apple' hoops. The person that is left without a hoop becomes the new lemon and has to go in the centre of the circle.

✦ If the name of another fruit is said out loud the same steps/ movements are done. If the word 'macedonia' is said, then everyone must get up and change places.

113. **Flick your button** 6+

Co-ordination/aim/agility   **Equipment:** *Chalk, buttons/counters*

✦ Mark out a 21cm square on the floor, and divide it into 9 equal squares, numbered 1 to 9. Draw a circle with a diameter of 7cm at each of the two top corners.

✦ From a distance of 1.5m away, the players must flick their buttons/counters towards the square using their thumb and either index or middle finger. Each player has three buttons (everyone takes it in turns to use the same buttons). Each player will flick all their buttons, one at a time. The numbers on the squares where the buttons fall are added up to give the total number of points that player has won.

✦ If the button falls on a line only half a point given; if it falls into one of the circles it will equal 10 points. The game is played in 5 rounds.

Index

Index